# LOVE IS BLOOD, LOVE IS FABRIC

## POEMS BY MARY DE LA FUENTE

atmosphere press

Published by Atmosphere Press

Cover art by C Naholnik
Cover design by Nick Courtright

Love is Blood, Love is Fabric
2020, Mary De La Fuente

atmospherepress.com

# LOVE IS BLOOD, LOVE IS FABRIC

# TABLE OF CONTENTS

## LOVE

## LOSS

## SEARCHING

## RETURN

## REBIRTH

LOVE

# I HAD SOMETHING TO TELL HIM

I had something to tell him,
                                something like the interstices
between tree branches at dawn and dusk,
the peak
                between the in-breath and the out,
a whisper formless and formed
                          only when his eyes,
his contours,

        evaded me.

# IF LOVE IS FABRIC, IF LOVE IS BLOOD

You stand under street lamps in a blue suede suit.
Take beating like a sparrow.

Beaming
>            rhizomes
>                        tree-tremored
>                                          under feet

Oozing
>            ink
>                        veined-wells
>                                          black street

You straighten your tie,
walk toward me.

*If love is fabric, if love is blood, what's me & you?*

You stare, through sparrow eyes,
something between us moves.

# WHEN I LOVED YOU

The day you wrote your number for me on a piece of tape,
onlookers shook their heads and whispered:
*She's gone off the deep end.*

You were raw, sullen, uninhibited.

You told me you were done trying to impress people.
You apologized for being so boring.
It's funny, that's why I admired you.

We'd sit on your porch in the fall.
Watch the leaves—red and orange—
scatter to the ground.

You asked me what it was like
to plan everything.

I didn't answer, only wanting
to hold you and soften the look in your eyes,
which were too still and too sad.

I didn't know that something too sweet
could start to taste bitter.
That I could open my heart in ways
that made me fear myself.

You tried to hurt me with words.
Told me, *You deserve better.*
*You should get out of this town.*

I did and never stopped thinking about you.

I could live in the most exotic place,
and still miss that spot on your steps,
the honor of your silence.

Now, sitting on my porch in the fall,
I listen to an empty street.

I didn't know how to tell you I love you.

Something like simplicity,
and the falling of leaves.

# TRAJECTORIES MEET

You were a man in a valley on his way up.
 I was receptive to a risk in its truest form.
   Trajectories meet.

I sense it flowing in my veins—
 this futile feeling,
   this current of untraversed hope.

It's a liquid that holds you & I:
 the syrup in a womb void
   trestles  wrapping  cocooned  coffins

# THE GRID AND THE FLAME

The way you interpret my speech:
your silences
tag onto my lapses in thought.
Then, my ticking silence,
your statement.

Whatever's between us
riles up in hard waves,
the intermingling of our thoughts
  mixing warm air and cold water
into something comforting.

Notes become more vibrant
when we're together,
after the upswing
that is our expectation
  and the downswing
of our contemplative sighs.

We spend long days enmeshed:
testing and compiling,
gathering, stoking
this fire we evoke together.

The grid and the flame
constantly scratching for connection,
waiting for that reverberating sound,
patient in the waiting.

# SILENCE

is where I feel at home with you.
Silence natural enough to sit in broad daylight,
where I let my gaze rest on your ocean canvas:
orange, red, stealth blue, bruised purple.

Your pipe balances on the dresser,
tepid from last night's use.

Plastic drapes cover the walls.
You tape them against the grain
where they meet the floor.

Paint brushes scatter to stab me
as I make my way to the bathroom.
Two Angry Bird toothbrushes
smudge white paste on the sink.

I walk to the bedroom
and see you hunched over,
knees on hard wood, a brush in your hands.

I wrap my arms around you from behind.
Whatever warmth I can offer, yours.

## PORTLAND ROYALTY

The smoke in your lungs & apartment
made me feel like I belonged to this city—
to reclusive bars and polluted air,
to people stripped of their glitzy armor.

Plastic chandeliers hung above white couches,
people in tinted mirrors chattered.

They all had their loves:
cigarettes, wine, sisters-in-law's, degrees.

I had your stare,
like we belonged next to dumpsters,
art walks, and start-up shops.

How did your severity, shyness—
your complete surrender to the black and grey—
make you a king among men?

# THE DARK BLOSSOMING

into too many parts,
<blockquote>
an underworld without walls,
infinite and echoing with reproach.
</blockquote>

Wanting too much,
flaming too much,

<blockquote>
reveling in all I don't know
& don't need to know.
</blockquote>

Too many shadows:

the kind after sleep,
the kind that hum
in the hollow of day.

# GOLDEN SKELETON

The black bed. The windows.  How you couldn't wait for summer so
    light would pour in on us naked, coated in each other's skin.

Me coming over, in a huff.  Cute, in your black t-shirt
with the holes, spelling Guns N Roses.

Sweet sadness. Meeting you always in a liquid embrace,
always at night, always wanting to stay above water.

My hair left curly, messy, unapologetic.
I could live off air food. I could see
straight through your white skin, your bones,
reminding me how fragile you were.

## II

The masks you made for us for the Halloween party.
I bailed. I was never a monster.  You agreed:
my eyes were too kind.

The woman in your painting, mouth open,
head wrenched upward as if by an invisible string
tied to her tongue. Desire glutted her face.
I wanted to be her, your riven queen.
You smelled like smoke. Your eyes were unmoving,
seeing though everything, unapologetic, haunting.

## III

On your porch, you held your hand out. I took it,
unthinking. Then against you. Then kissing you.
Your wall hard, your bed soft, my breathing ragged,
my sobs happy.

## IV

How did I survive the orange hair on your chest, the tattoo colors:
the love birds, the cages, the rose and bullet guns,
the black lettering around your hips? Your sharp hips hurt me.
I fit inside your boundaries sideways.
I could never get to your head.

The bumps of your vertebrae, the way your pants fell
when you did chin ups in the living room, the time you rocked me on
    the bathroom floor, blackout drunk.

Your stares from the kitchen window in the restaurant
of my first low-wage job, the blood that roiled underneath my skin,
    my retreat into the shamed hallway.

Writing your name on a piece of tape, the night
you asked me out for the first time. Kissing me, pulling my hair
in the winter night against my car in the restaurant parking lot,
reaching the wetness gushing, the shock I had never experienced.

The concert. The men were animals. You in the mosh pit:
the skeleton grew blood and guts, white lines and spinning limbs.

The night you put your hand on my leg, the night
we were already broken, the night I still didn't know
how to tell myself to learn discipline, to unlearn the steps
to your house, the experience that taught me more would only
    destroy the perfect picture I had of you in my head.

## V

The agony, the stone hard resolve, not to drive to your house,
not to call. You saying we want to be more than we are.

## VI

Months later, pulling you to my chest, feeling that same
white hot light in my head; persistent, bright, steady.
I love you. Always did—before we met, when I first saw you,

all the nights at your house, at mine, together, alone,
contemplating the dark underworld I could travel with you
if we were dead, if it was allowed. What amount of time together or
apart would satisfy this? Does growing up mean
no longer loving what tears you apart?

# THE BOY'S LOST

You open to me a razor-faced boy in chains,
screaming from down beneath your iris,
the brown swallowing him there like molasses.
Looking at your paintings,
the boy softens, opens.  An almond sheen.
You grab me and the boy's lost.
Cursive fingertips over moon-bumped skin.
You know me without touching me,
know what I long for beyond the lies of my mouth.
Where has not-having
& not-knowing this gone?

# WAITING

You say *I have to get out of the house.*

You do and I'm left,
circling feet over tile,
dancing.

Miasma of carbon fumes.
It's always cold here.
Deep in the basement a song wells—
up here, I listen.

To earthy sighs and spaces
between the walking in and walking out.
Light rays on guttered walls
where no sleep can bathe.

A whiteness where hot stones have pressed—
to the surface of my mouth,
to the arching of my back.

This song whispers, grazing me
with translucence,
silk in bottomless jars of fleas,

waiting for you to come home.

LOSS

# WHEN WE BROKE APART

We trusted with veils over our faces
& train tracks chalked on our hearts.
We wanted healing.
Our wounds re-opened when we broke apart—
had to face ourselves anew.
Me, amazed for years after our contact.
What it was to love you.

# IF HOPE CAN BE BRUISED

a blow to the stomach,
full moon to crescent moon;
  no relief of new moon

a fledgling prepares for liftoff:
searches for completeness,
  plunges into darkness

## PURPLE-COLORED STAINS

You were clean inside,
would never conceive of my lies,
my actions: purple-colored stains,
coagulations inside my heart.
I was already halfway down the way,
and I couldn't turn back.
Even if I could, if I were able to stand
at the line on the other side,
there'd still be something inside me,
egging me onward.
But this: I couldn't be satisfied here, now,
because of the terrible notion
that came with having crossed it.

## I CANNOT BE

I cannot be the rails under your wreck.
I cannot love again without going back.
The resounding between us:
human potential / human weakness—
both and beyond both.
More and more I think of you as a conspiracist,
our time as a blink.
Only in dreams are you there,
silent, holding up your hands and crying,
tugging on my mesh-mess heart.
Your presence / our contact
an explosion of angry bees
        my cheek on your cheek
venom as they sting

# RECOGNITION

I know the click-clack of your shoes,
the tattering of uncertain breath,
how it tugs air between us.
What will it take to know you?

# I AM JUST ONE BODY IN THE BED

What was your shape?
Muscles long and sinewy or short and bulky?
Was your thumb calloused or smooth
as it trailed my flesh in cursive stripes?

Was your face dim
or lit from inside, shielded by snakeskin?
Your touch. Was it impatient or greedy,
pressing me up tight against the wall?

Images I fuzz as they up-spring in mind:
spread, dissolve.

You were blaze and caution,
seeping water into me at night,
enfolding me in feathers:
a long-ago home.

Squeeze me
       You
              Breathe harder, deeper
       triangular mouth, light fissures
       a snake body moves between us
            curving
            cramped

I don't know your knuckles
Your breath
Your blush at dawn
Your hunting eyes

Greyed memory.

I weep because of this:
rich knowledge,
thick as syrup—
scratching sorrow.

## WOLF

What is off?
Day cycles:
desperation, sweaty expectation, dry hope.

Night
      overtakes
              sun's peached embroidery in blue-tinted sky.
      Despair. Neon-green and malice black.
      Sliver of silver moonlight—release.

Here I change. I match the night. Hungry—
a star-gazing wolf, intent on her prey.
You're not here.  Memory dim.

                  Greedy for movement
                      Atonement of bodies
                          Stories we tell

                        Freedom to move
                  within realms
            of acuities
      & attachments

            Contact, then—quiet.  Numb inside.
            Chewing  dead  stains
                  inside.

Strength of other / weakness of self.
Strength of self
Release of self

# DIARY OF LONGING

The restaurant on a cliff,
            the entryway at the top of a winding set of stairs,
                        the wood ascending up the side of a steep hill.

Only the workers enter through here,
            and in the small den that leads the way to the kitchen,
                        the place where *he* stares out at me,
                                    the servers drink and get drunk.

I stand outside.
            Pacing, waiting for a reason, an excuse,
                                                to go inside,
                                                            talk to him.

At the moment I give up, I'm face to face with him,
                        our breath coming in hot spurts.

Inside his apartment, the television on. It makes a low humming sound above our heads. He takes me by the elbow to a cot. My skin soft and velvety as I bend over forward, the arch of my back sleek and inviting. He's on top of me, touching my body, stroking it. I think of the window. Who's peering in? The boy looks in at us but cannot see us, his mouth forming a perfect *O.* I feel his desperation; I'm heavy with need.

*He* turns away from me. I ache.
He lifts his hands from my breasts.
My breath goes out like a whoosh
of falling sleet. He gets up off the cot,
the movement jarring me up & then down.
My hand reaches out for him; my body
hums over the creak of the bed. He won't
hear my moans, won't look at my face.

26

My pleadings are silent. Killing me:
bruises ripened by his refusal.
*His* fragile leanings, *his* world of silent
emotion—never mine.

In a moment, I'm back behind the
winding steps in my father's house.
*He's* leaning on the wall, reaching for
me, hips relaxed, mouth bending
down to mine. I hear voices. *They'll
find us.* I flush again with desire. A
need so big I feel the legions in my
heart walls split. They tear open,
exposing a gorge where my heart
should be. The blood overwhelms us
both. It pours from my chest as I walk
away. My head swings in both
directions. We hadn't kissed but the
cords of our reciprocal tensions met,
intermingled and said something,
wanted something. *When will they
come?*

I awake.
I'd never made it past the den to the kitchen.
We didn't sleep together on the cot.
My disease:
I left him without glancing back, rushed out of that room,
fecal with sweat, my mouth dry,
longing, longing, longing.
The thing I cannot have.

The need stays with me          all day.
                                I sit, contemplate going to his house,
contemplate the ways          this would tear my life apart.
Go home.                        Eat chicken soup from the can.
Sit on my bed and get drunk.   Just to call him, just to hear his voice.

I wait on a dead line,          wait to hear the scratchiness of his words,
the laziness in them.           Picture his slow, lumbering walk,

27

the motor of his hips.

I dial again and hang up. Put the phone down

Then again eight more times.

I decide on tomorrow, make a grocery list,

walk outside to get the mail.　　Write a letter to him and rip it up.


What is this nagging in my head for,

what purpose does it serve?

I drop my head to my pillow.


In the morning feel the tense　　revival　of muscles.
See his black bedroom shaded　before my eyes,
walk to the bathroom.

Feel the tug of the never-ending ache
and know　　　　　　　　I'd dreamt
of him　　　　　　　　　again.

# X MAN

You had held up your arms to make an X over your face.
I'd spent hours, it seemed, asking faceless people    *Where does he live?*
        *Was this his car?*                        *Does he live with lions?*

        *Lions and dogs*, they said.

I walked into your den on stilts.
Stared at the ceiling, how high it was.              There was a ladder.
        I climbed, looked out over a railing, you came home.

Stepped inside, eyes shot up to mine.
                        You did the X thing with your hands

in a moment I was close to you,
could smell the soap and leather pomade you used,
eyes averted, you were angry.            Not angry.

        The thing on your face was an aimless,            nameless angst.

The heat between us was a rasp
I wanted to throw everything down at your feet and cry out
        but something held me back;

        I wanted to grab at your hands—a heedless grip.

I wanted to scream, to gouge out your center chest,
but you left me in that stale stench of want
and went away again into the kitchen.

        In a moment I was back at the top of the stairs.

With one sweep of your head upward,
your face unforgiving
and crusted over with ferity,

you let your snarling, slandering dog loose on me.
It bounded up the stairs
        and the fear and the power and the enormity of the thing

        grew as you shrunk in the peripheral,
                your stance collapsed inward again, closed.

# BETRAYAL?

You say I left you for someone else, but it's not people leaving people, it's people searching God through people. And God doesn't dull once he's been found; God is past and future, the spark in all man, the amalgam of me and you and him. How would you understand this, and how would I explain? It's not you I discarded, but the me I was with you, then. And it's not him I wanted, but my soul. I still want my soul. I will always want my soul.

SEARCHING

## WHAT I WANT

If only I could turn back thoughts
unto themselves,
until a new birth conforms
to the misgivings of the past.
Is it not darkness that drives us?

# EDGAR ALLAN POE

*The way my heart stops and starts*
*For whatever it is that it wants.*

I see the circles set in your pale face,
your dark eyes a frazzled blue,
eyebrows unruly and furrowed.

I read your short stories:
a heart thumps under creaking
floorboards, an old man sways to
the sound of the clock on the wall,
the blades of a chair curve over
chiseled wood.  Your mind needs
catastrophe and a silent room.

I think you,
with your melancholy eyes,
moustache & clouded mind,
could understand why my heart
stops & starts
for whatever it is that it wants.

## AT FAMILY GET-TOGETHERS,
### I'M THE ONE WHO

looks at tree silhouettes as everyone speaks,
wonder if everyone is as indebted to conversation
as they are to other aspects of their lives,
is not guarded enough
to protect against rash remarks and negativity,
isn't attached enough to adhere much care,
is always in this lonely space
of mind fire and feigned presence

## I WISH I COULD BE

like the baristas,
wild in their surrender to nothingness,
  untethered,
holding the vibrancy—
urgency—that comes
from not desiring anything at all.

Eyes half-lidded,
laughter stout and flippant,
their bodies energies of singularity,
  perpetual echoes
of inner and outer ghosts.

They lived on the brink
and in the barest of ways,
each thought extending
only to the lip of the next movement.
They drank and their eyes glossed over,
  became a word in the dark—

animals nebulous in red flashes,
lips cracking for next sip,
hands swarming over impulses,
over friends and lovers,
fingers licking for lack of want,
curling at their sides.

Ablaze with the rust of reality sparked:
so much wanting satisfied.
Breathing the grime of place,
wandering in-between walls,
  creating ceaselessly

# HOG VS. MAN

The club's lights are how I remember them, green and silvery like varicose veins spreading feverishly over the ceiling. Multi-colored shimmering's of a chandelier. The hog's head mantled in the foyer above a looming bookcase. Beyond this, laying slack and restless in their folds are curtains the color of mahogany. Somber and forgotten like the edges of a vignette lost to lights, flickering and fast on the dancers, emboldening them with shadow, making gaudy their creamed skin. The hog haunts me. A snout that pokes out at visitors, tusks riling upward and slashing. In its eyes, remnants. The last snapshot of beast as it regards man: a brilliant reflection of rage.

# KWAME

I know he's well attuned to everything around him.
I know because for our Kind Words project he said to me:
*Sometimes you are nice. Sometimes you are mean.*

He'd wait outside the door, even after the bell rang.
He'd flip his chair over in class and tell me off.

He made fun of the Disney movies the class loved.

*That's beautiful!* he'd exclaim,
after we sat through an emotional song
belted by a Disney teen pop star
in full red lipstick and purple streaked hair.

*Ooooooh! You just got told by a WOMAN!*
he'd say after I told his friends to get to class.

His sarcasm earned him some laughs.
Once I'd made the whole class turn and stare.
*Kwame wants some attention.*

Then came our table talks where'd I'd ask him about his family
and what he'd like to do when he grew up.
He felt comfortable enough, I guess, to fill me in.

He used to bang his too-big boots through the halls
and imitate other teachers marching into their rooms.

I was impressed once when he came to school
in a white linen button-up shirt instead of his usual uniform.
*You look great today,* I told him.

I smiled when he came in before the bell,
felt my heart break when he cried about his sister.
We'd play hide-and-seek and wait for his mom after school.

He didn't know how to write kind notes for our Kind Words project.
Another student who barely talked to him all year wrote him a letter:

38

Kwame you are cool. You are funny. You are from Africa.
I don't know anything about Africa. I like your clothes they are fresh.
Raúl

Kwame came back from speech lessons with a grin on his face.
*Watch me read!*
He'd sit at my table and move a finger under the words in our textbook.

Once I let him see my tears because I was so proud.
He didn't get embarrassed after that,
he came back to read too.

I played it off like I didn't care too much. I think he knew.

# MELANCHOLY AS THE TRAILS BENEATH MAN

Train tracks flee under a metal motor.
I sit in the cabin at dusk, feel my labored breath.

Malaria and generals who mutter piety
                    and speak only of the entitlement of their race.
Here I am, dozing and light-headed,
                    remembering the evenings of broiled crabs and
biscuit dinners,
                    sensing at once the rumbling of my stomach,
the aimlessness of my spindly limbs,
                    the curving of my spine against cushion seat;
notice melancholy, un-named,
                    lodged at the base of my throat.

Generations have gotten me here. Horrors.
Miseries, beatings, men sick after oiled-rice & egg smorgasbords.
Instead of desensitizing, becomes all: explains all.
Jealousy, rage, deceit
all spring from an endless well.

Only the *scale* of absurdity, the *scale*   of violence varies.
It's in all, waiting to erupt,                to be incited.

   I.   Weary. Feel tremors of transgression like they're my own.
Dreams, snapshots—how they appear, in sleeping and waking.
Their heaviness, how they sit inside my flesh. Rage. I felt it shiver
through the gunman's hand: the impulse to erase. The desire to
flourish one's own image. Demarcation, an altar crimson.
This body, this enslavement.

Atrocities of history, all inside me now,
for I'm made of / filled with memory.
Reverberating. I expand, know it.
Can name it, cannot conquer it. Just is.

                    What about that love feeling, my first love?

The me that died before it ended? That trust,
that severity, that youthful fever; all gone,
and while I'm still young?

I tell myself this: absence I must let go of.
Abscess gone.
I need to spring forth! Into new voids &
spur life.

How could I? Bring new life to this scarcity,
this warped melancholy of continual
striving?

Sadness seduces sadness.
Life bleeds sadness.

The nuances of suffering, the terrible
trails beneath man. Me: in frivolity—
in a different world then,
a fake and enterprising world—

and me, here, now, aware of just how sick I
feel at the moment, of who I am if made from
this muck, of who I'm not & must become,
diligently, sorrowfully, obediently, to escape
this pain of melancholy.

# HE CALLED ME ANGEL

Tarot reader said I am straight from mystic world
He called me angel

Do angels bleed their white robes?
Knife / pursuit / a feeling like scalpel

Flesh over veins / tendons
Pillage a white night

Trees brighter / people scrambling
Walk faster / toes / push / off-ground

Prowling guests of imagination
Give me one lucid thought / one incisive action

Lone reptile / atone / bury me
Body on the bed / a reedy stalk / green shoot forced out

This sludge / this straining
Beauty rough / rigged / tarred lines / stab out light

Deep as you can / cut / awake shaking shard glass
See me / come into me / give everything

It's a curse / a putrid ice-life
Hard / restless / fighter father

Give me your all / detritus / I pick up
Energies troubling / tenor trembling

Dissect me / effusion of blood
Render complete / this non-knowledge

This gift you gave / prisms glint gold
Hurt as beauty / hurt as wholeness

Give me whatever's between no / thing and some / thing
Bring me absolution / (ac)complice / shhh / they hear us

## DAVID (FROM ERNEST HEMINGWAY'S *THE GARDEN OF EDEN*)

David fell in love with Catherine
on the golden beach in Cannes
until she cropped her hair short
like his.

It was while they were in the café
with absinthe they met Marita.
Catherine had her first,
then David.

Who are we to love more
than one / two at once, or hate
ourselves, and catch our
reflections as they pass by?

## BODY LIKE AN EEL

Throat gurgle / breath before contact
Body like an eel / hips rotate / meet mine

Dirtied mind / auctioned touch / lurch

I'll take you now / blast of heel / death as life
meet me outside this bent roiled earth

Work wrong till it breaks you / dulls you
Last year's pollen charged as / light particles giving
Worn skin / hog teeth / blare under / Saturn eyes

What is it I want?
Explode / each second / each ounce / each cell

Teach me how to live / like this
Splice / blaze / pique
Exuberance a contusion / always hungry

# YOU WERE NOT LIKE THAT MAN

You were not like that man.
That man had one dial
Mind cluttered from inside out
Repeat: *What'd I say?*
*Tell me, what'd I say?*
 *I didn't kill him.*

You raged against
What'd been taken

A fistful of hair
Spittle of spit on corner lip,
Eyes wider than could perceive
The sphere, the globe, the failings
Before you
In you

Rage against what's been lost
Rage against the muddle
A blaze wild
Brusque temper / tie too white
 for contours
 for the single dial

# IF ONLY I WERE YOUR OBSESSION

If only I were a black swan made of glass—
the centerpiece in a forest gilded with moss.
Or a dragon, my mouth spitting pink jewel-stars
into a sapphire dusk,
longing for a skeleton atop a grave.

I'd live as my intemperate self,
the part of me that wants too much,
that wants you to consume me,
        all the while
looking at my reflection in your eyes.

I'd slump, melt, crack and shatter,
sink into what you don't say:
        your fire
                        my frost ice—
slip out again so I can draw out your need.

What parts of me crave scrutiny,
        need
                *you*
                        to see?

# IT WAS LONELY,

but I needed the loneliness, the silence of trees and moss and sky. There was in it a stillness I longed for, a span of time without the crust of responsibility, the interloping manipulations of association. It was during these times I thought of you, how you'd engulf me in one of your hugs, the warmth I craved. How could they end so abruptly, our adventures? Why couldn't I love the person I loved most? Then, this question: was there an end to this? Or would it be ache and rise, ache and rise, until the pain was so dull it sat in my bones, their creaking sounding my growing age, the hurts I'd learned to soothe out?

## THE SPACE BETWEEN PERCEIVABILITY
## AND THOUGHT

The contemplativeness that is the thoughtful life
& makes living such a dream
Invents a romantic sustainability:
knowing you're alive,
knowing you possess beauty,
wishing you were more of this beauty

# GOOD AND STRONG

Lost.
Can't point fingers to evil lurking.
Its form found—


      strengthens from inside-out.


A level releases.

She bends over the toilet,
spine splinters up the back.

              A vault cracks open
              Levers pop
              Combustion.

Good  strong  bone  you  are.

## JUDGEMENT

After some time of growing accustomed to night, I started wondering how to relate to others / how to proceed / how long could I go on spurning the day, which to me meant time. Time without the light of judgement, discernment, mind. I needed that judgement, wanted it; I was losing my walls, my conditions to what I thought my life was and how I believed it to be in past and future. I wanted to regain my voice, establish my place in the world, have a name. That's always the thing, isn't it? This feeling, this knowing, this love—still outside.

# HEALING

The healing between us is what will heal the world.

What alchemizes at the smallest,
most infinitesimal levels will send waves,
through and through, up and over the greatest of heights,
will transmute modest things and one-on-one interactions
until the entire world will know itself the way I knew you.

*If love is fabric, if love is blood, what is truth?*

RETURN

# SPARROW

Exhaustion makes you soft,
sets a blanket of melancholy on your features.

How beautiful you are,
toiling away,
carrying this mantle of grief and guilt,
finding the strength to come here, and now.

The disorientation that marks a constant fatigue,
a willingness to be bound under insurmountable weight.

 To not know the heaviness of the thing you carry,
just that you need to carry it.

no awareness of being watched,
 of being admired,

> of being the subject of anything other
> than a passing event
> embedded in a time
> you did not know you created.

## THE KISS

I'd been imagining it into existence before this night. I had observed the directions, shadows, dialects of his face, his expressions, his mannerisms. Elicited memories: a phantasmagoria of these same dispositions, enfolded, molded, engraved—snippets from times past. Only then, with schematic folds unfurling before my eyes, I, by tuning into this turbulence, saw him enlarged, intensified, his multidimensionality catapulted tenfold into my every sense, solidifying in every second through our transference. The dials in him were made clearer to me. Their effects on me were profound, but no more profound than our first meeting. There was instead a new fluidity to our correspondence, to the waxing and waning of our true selves, now more apparent, gilded: a sheen illuminating the rods of our bodies clasped together. A whirlpool illuminating two facades anteriorly drenched in shadows.

## WHAT'S NOT CONJURED

I felt good then, walking this way when you walked that. The burning that came into me when I lay alone in my bed, the imaginings of your face down and eyes closed and me pressing my lips to your forehead, your nose, your lips.

I grasp again for that image, the one that presented itself and not the one I conjured, the one that was so willingly and earnestly giving. It was me that wanted to give to you, soothe you, look on you, but more than that, protect you. Me—glorified in having a focus, a specimen, a human soul which offered so much deliverance.

# REBIRTH

# THE THING ABOUT DREAMS

*They're a half-truth. Represent either side of the moon: intuition or illusion, fear.*
*What if everything we wish for is already in the process of becoming?*

## I REALIZED WHY HE'D NEVER SPOKEN TO ME ABOUT LOVE

It had a way of sweeping through his every action. How could he talk to me about something as sweeping as his own life? My own love, that which had enraged me, then unsettled me, was now the undulation I carried into the every day. I fell asleep to its murmur. How was it possible? To love someone so completely, you realize suddenly and sharply how alone you were before? And now you're sunk in this love: hammocked by its juices, intertwined in its burdens. Have no choice but to become more than yourself.

# WORDS & SPACES

You said I focused too much on words,
and you, the spaces between them.

*Music isn't like literature,* you said.
*You don't see the words written down on the page.*
*There aren't any spaces between them, they flit by too fast.*

The cornbread muffins I made:
you hesitated, didn't want them,
smashed your face into their soft centers & cried.

I kissed your tears one by one,
saw the way your eyes enlarged:
the child in your face, the teenager, the adult.

The entire night drenched
on the mast of your silhouette.

You said, *Where is your proof?*
And me: *Isn't everything the becoming of an idea?*

You told me to stand up for my dreams,
believe in them, even if they didn't include you.

You learned to swallow when things got tough.
I opted to scream.

Our bike rides at night—
skittish laughter, dodging frogs.

That ride you held your hand at my back.
My pants stuck in the spokes & you fell.

That night you pushed my sickness,
barehanded, down the drain.

You spoke in broken English so you wouldn't lose your identity.

I learned your language to expand on mine.

Why couldn't you hear
the things I was trying to say in my tongue?

When I left, I said, *I would sacrifice for you.*
You heard, *I don't love you.*

You told me you'd be the bridge to anything I wanted.
Then, with that pinch of hurt residing so delicately in your features,
asked, *Why are you so scared to love me?*

You said your brother was the prized son,
won first place in the national biking competition.

Everyone complimented him
on his likeness to your dad.

But you planned his service,
stayed up with him,
held his hand on the night of his death.

You'd say it wasn't time yet,
so we'd sit in your car, people watch.
You'd walk me to my door, kiss me under fluorescent lights.

I wanted to hold you but wouldn't.
Pulled back to allow you that space
to move toward me again.

Us meeting each other and breaking away,
our breath shared and tentative:

desire robed as caution,
honor masking our mimicry of internal questions.

You asked, *Don't you want to be happy?*
I told you I wanted to grow.

You wanted the peace that warrants peace.

I wanted peace fought for.

Your father told you, *Do something Mexico needs.*
Sharpened that look you had
that saw straight and un-straight.

When we married,
your mind started its calculations
of how you'd give, what more you'd do.

All I could think about
was how people don't belong to people,
so why did we?

When we divorced
you wouldn't let me touch you.
You pushed back your shoulders. Lifted your chin. Said,

*I love you. I won't ever hate you. I couldn't.*
*Don't be ashamed. Look at me.*

Your eyes rimmed with red, hands tucked between your knees.

You needed that space
            between          words

Between Hurts

Silence got me here,
to that place of knowing
the only spaces that needed dissolving were in myself.

And now,

            there's white space all over
                                    this page of poetry

            that fails

To tribute you

With words,          With spaces

# A THING NAMELESS, SHAPELESS

Sometimes, I think maybe it's wrong,
egotistical even, to place so much emphasis on one individual.
That's oneness—there's power in it.
When I start seeing you, or rather,
the love I have for you in everyone and everything,
I know I'm on the right track.

Plus—the nagging purple bruise. Egging me onward.
*Cross the line*, it says. *Defy all odds.*
I laugh at it. Curse it.
My feet are moving, and there's a singularity to it.
There's a thing nameless, shapeless—
that when I learn to let go, like you say—
will come back to me.

## ACKNOWLEDGEMENTS

I wish to acknowledge the editors of the following publications in which these poems, or a version of these poems, have appeared:

*San Diego Poetry Annual:* "Golden Skeleton," "At Family Get-Togethers, I'm the One Who," "If Hope Can Be Bruised," and "Binghamton Royalty" (new version: "Portland Royalty").

*The Carousel Issue 6:* "My Obsession," "The Boy's Lost," "I Cannot Be," and "Good Strong Bone you Are" (new version: "Good and Strong").

*Art Ascent & Literature Journal Issue 33:* "When I Loved You."

# ABOUT ATMOSPHERE PRESS

Atmosphere Press is an independent, full-service publisher for excellent books in all genres and for all audiences. Learn more about what we do at atmospherepress.com.

We encourage you to check out some of Atmosphere's latest releases, which are available at Amazon.com and via order from your local bookstore:

*The Unordering of Days,* poetry by Jessica Palmer

*It's Not About You,* poetry by Daniel Casey

*A Dream of Wide Water,* poetry by Sharon Whitehill

*Radical Dances of the Ferocious Kind,* poetry by Tina Tru

*The Woods Hold Us,* poetry by Makani Speier-Brito

*My Cemetery Friends: A Garden of Encounters at Mount Saint Mary in Queens, New York,* nonfiction and poetry by Vincent J. Tomeo

*Report from the Sea of Moisture,* poetry by Stuart Jay Silverman

*The Enemy of Everything,* poetry by Michael Jones

*The Stargazers,* poetry by James McKee

*The Pretend Life,* poetry by Michelle Brooks

*Minnesota and Other Poems,* poetry by Daniel N. Nelson

*Interviews from the Last Days,* sci-fi poetry by Christina Loraine

*the oneness of Reality,* poetry by Brock Mehler

# ABOUT THE AUTHOR

Mary De La Fuente earned a Master of Arts in English with a concentration in creative writing from Binghamton University in 2018. Her work has appeared in the *The Carousel Issue 61, Art Ascent & Literature Journal Issue 33,* and the *San Diego Poetry Annual* 2014-15, 2015-16, 2016-17, 2017-18, and 2018-19. Her poem, "Pull-n-Peel Licorice Twists" was selected as a finalist  for The Poet's Billow 2017 Atlantis Award. Mary is a former preschool and second-grade teacher for the San Antonio Independent School District in Texas and works as a copywriter in New York.

9 781636 495248